ANIMALS
That Make a Difference!

Bees
벌

Ashley Lee &
Jared Siemens

Explore other books at:
WWW.ENGAGEBOOKS.COM

VANCOUVER, B.C.

𝓮 WWW.ENGAGEBOOKS.COM

Bees: Level 1 Bilingual (English/Korean) (영어/한국어)
Animals That Make a Difference!
Lee, Ashley 1995 —
Siemens, Jared 1989 —
Text © 2021 Engage Books
Edited by: A.R. Roumanis
and Lauren Dick
Translated by: Gio Oh
Proofread by: Tamara Kazali

Text set in Arial Regular.
Chapter headings set in Arial Black.

FIRST EDITION / FIRST PRINTING

LIBRARY AND ARCHIVES CANADA CATALOGUING IN PUBLICATION

LIBRARY AND ARCHIVES CANADA CATALOGUING IN PUBLICATION

Title: Animals That Make a Difference: Bees Level 1 Bilingual (English/Korean) (영어/한국어)
Names: Jared Siemens, author

ISBN 978-1-77476-451-0 (hardcover)
ISBN 978-1-77476-450-3 (softcover)

Subjects:
LCSH: Bees—Juvenile literature
LCSH: Human-animal relationships—Juvenile literature

Classification: LCC QL565.2 .S54 2020 | DDC J595.79/9—DC23

Contents
목차

What Are Bees?
벌은 무엇인가요?

Bees are flying insects.
An insect is a small animal
without a backbone.
벌은 날아다니는
곤충이에요. 곤충은
척추가 없는 작은
동물이에요.

An insect's skeleton is on the outside of its body.
곤충의 뼈대는 몸 밖에 있어요.

What Do Bees Look Like?
벌은 어떻게 생겼나요?

Bees have fuzzy hair on their bodies.
They are mostly black and yellow.
벌의 몸은 보송보송한 털로 덮여 있어요.
그 털은 대부분 검정색이나 노란색입니다.

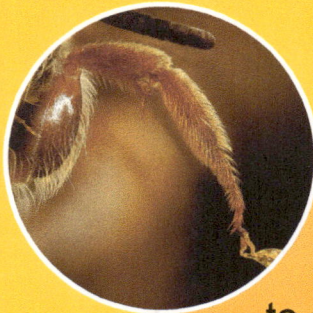

Bees have six
legs. They use
their front legs
to clean their head.
벌의 다리는 6개에요. 앞발은
머리를 씻는데 사용해요.

Bees have four wings. These wings make a buzzing sound when bees fly.

벌의 날개는 4개에요. 이 날개들이 벌이 날아다닐때 위잉 소리를 낸답니다.

Female bees have a stinger. Male bees do not have a stinger.

암컷 벌은 침을 가지고 있어요. 수컷 벌은 침이 없답니다.

Where Do Bees Live?
벌은 어디서 사나요?

Bees live in large groups called colonies.
These colonies live in nests called hives.
벌은 무리를 이뤄 다녀요. 이 무리는
벌집이라고 부르는 둥지에서 살아요.

Most beehives are home
to about 60,000 bees.
보통 벌집은 60,000마리
벌들의 집이에요.

Bees live in every part of the world. Blue banded bees come from Australia. Cape honey bees live in South Africa. Rock honey bees are mainly found in Nepal.
벌은 전세계 곳곳에 살고있답니다. 푸른띠 벌은 호주에서 왔어요. 케이프 꿀벌은 남아프리카에 살아요. 바위꿀벌은 주로 네팔에서 찾을 수 있어요.

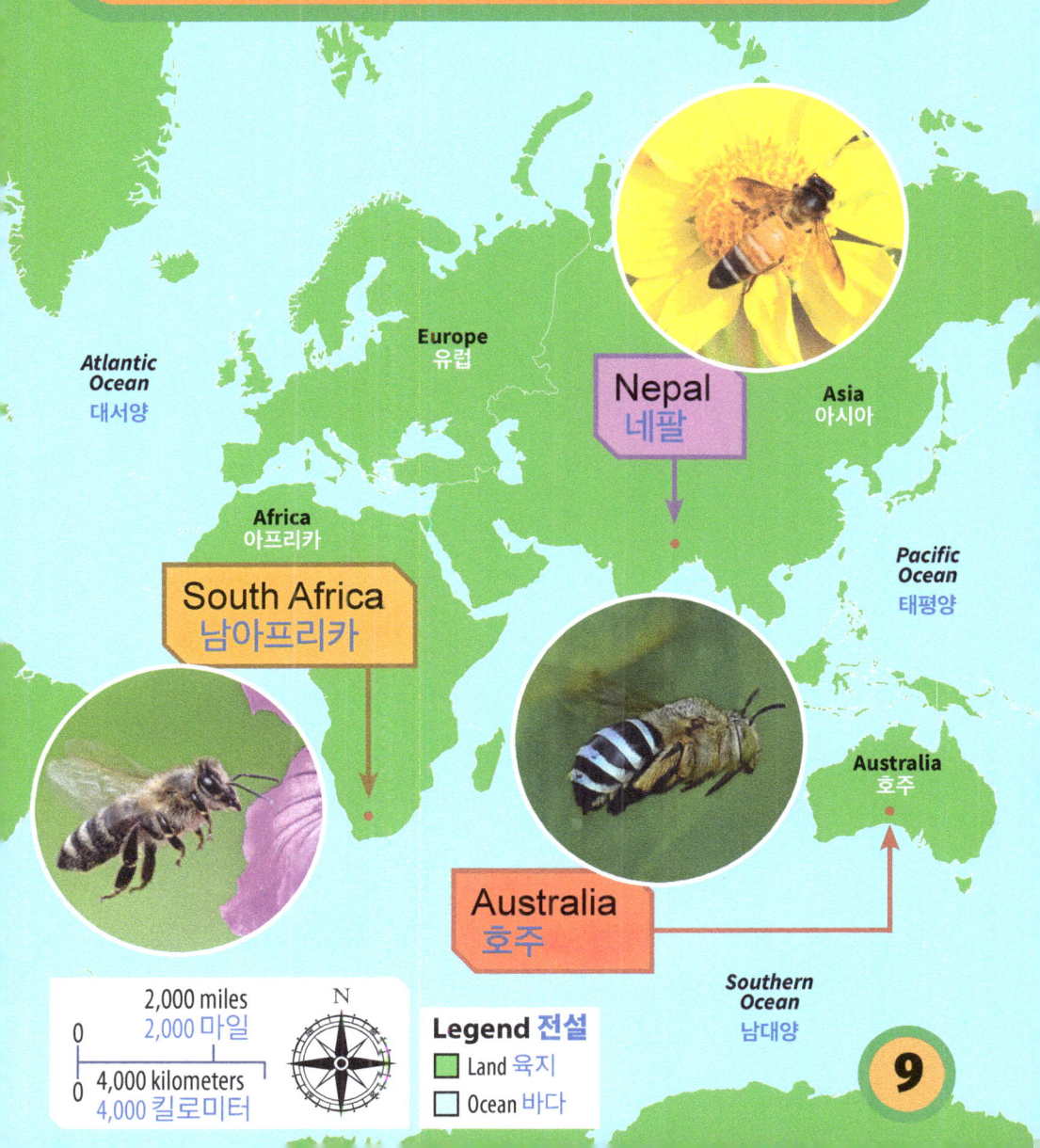

Europe
유럽

Atlantic
Ocean
대서양

Nepal
네팔

Asia
아시아

Africa
아프리카

South Africa
남아프리카

Pacific
Ocean
태평양

Australia
호주

Australia
호주

Southern
Ocean
남대양

2,000 miles
2,000 마일

N

4,000 kilometers
4,000 킬로미터

Legend 전설
Land 육지
Ocean 바다

9

What Do Bees Eat?
벌은 무엇을 먹나요?

Bees eat pollen and nectar from flowers. Pollen is a kind of fine powder that flowers make. Nectar is a kind of sweet liquid flowers make.

벌은 꽃가루나 꽃에서 나오는 꿀을 먹어요.
꽃가루는 꽃에서 나오는 고운 가루에요.
꿀은 꽃에서 나오는 달콤한 액체에요.

Bees have a special tongue that works like a straw. This lets them drink water and nectar.

벌은 빨때처럼 생긴 신기한 혀를 가지고 있어요. 이걸로 물이나 꿀을 마신답니다.

How Do Bees Talk to Each Other?
벌은 서로 어떻게 이야기하나요?

Bees talk to each other using special smells. These smells are called pheromones.

벌은 특별한 향을 사용해 서로 이야기를 합니다. 이 향은 페로몬이라고 불러요.

Bees have wires on their heads called antennae. They use their antennae to smell pheromones.

벌의 머리에는 더듬이라고 불리는 선이 있어요. 벌은 더듬이를 사용해 페로몬을 맡습니다.

Bee Life Cycle
벌의 일생

Bees have four stages in their life cycle. These stages are egg, larva, pupa, and adult. Queen bees lay all the eggs in a hive. The eggs hatch into larva after about 3 days.

벌은 4단계의 삶의 단계가 있어요. 단계는 알, 애벌레, 번데기, 성체로 나누어요. 여왕벌이 벌집에서 알을 낳아요. 3일뒤 알들은 애벌레로 부화해요.

Larvae grow for about 6 to 9 days.
애벌레는 6,9일동안 자랍니다.

Larvae turn into pupae. They hide inside hard shells called cocoons. All of their body parts grow at this time.

애벌레는 번데기로 자라요
애벌레는 고치라고 불리는
딱딱한 껍데기안에 숨어요.
몸의 모든 부분이 이때 자랍니다.

Pupae become adults after about 21 days. Adult bees have different jobs. Worker bees gather food. Drone bees help the queen bee make more eggs.

번데기는 21일 이후 성체가
됩니다. 어른벌은 다른 일이
있어요. 일벌은 먹이를
모아요. 숫벌은 여왕벌이
많은 알을 생산할 수 있게 도와요.

Curious Facts About Bees

Bees can fly up to
20 miles (32 kilometers)
per hour.
벌은 한시간에
20마일(32킬로미터)
까지 날 수 있어요.

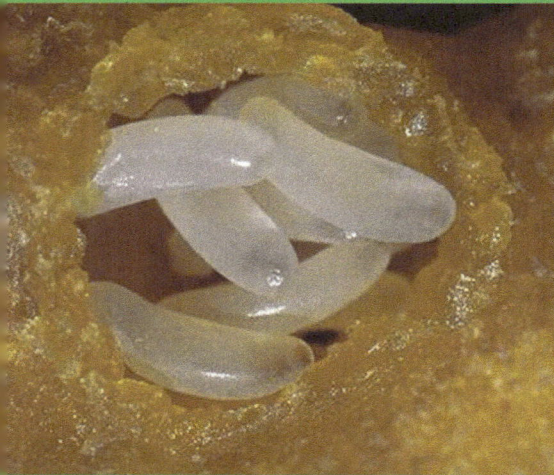

Queen bees lay around
1,500 eggs per day.
여왕벌은 하루에
1,500개의 알을
낳을 수 있어요.

A bee can use its two
front feet to taste things.
벌은 앞발 2개로
맛을 볼 수 있어요.

벌에 대한 흥미로운 사실들

Most bees visit 50 to 100 flowers before they go back to the hive.
대부분 벌들은 벌집으로 돌아가기전 50개에서 100개의 꽃에 찾아갑니다.

It takes about 12 bees their entire lives to make just one teaspoon of honey.
1숟가락의 꿀을 만들기위해 12마리의 벌이 평생을 일해야합니다.

A bee's wings flap between 12,000 and 15,000 times each minute.
벌의 날개는 1분동안 12,000번에서 15,000 펄럭일 수 있습니다.

17

Kinds of Bees
벌의 종류

There are more than 20,000 different kinds of bees. Honeybees, bumblebees, carpenter bees, and killer bees are some of the most common.
세상에는 20,000종 이상의 다른 벌들이 있습니다. 꿀벌, 호박벌, 목수벌, 살인벌이 제일 흔한 벌입니다.

Killer bees are known to chase people if upset. They are not more dangerous than other bees.
살인벌은 화가 나면 사람들을 쫓아다닌다고 알려져 있어요. 하지만 다른 벌들보다 특별히 더 위험하지는 않아요.

Bumblebees have fuzzy
black and yellow bodies.
호박벌은 보송보송한 검정색
노란색 몸을 가졌습니다.

Carpenter bees are mostly
black. They make nesting
holes in wood.
목수벌은 보통 까맣습니다.
목수벌은 보통 나무에 구멍을
뚫어 둥지를 만듭니다.

Honeybees are golden
yellow. They have dark
brown stripes.
꿀벌은 금빛 노란색이에요.
꿀벌은 어두운 갈색
줄무늬가 있어요.

How Bees Help Earth
벌이 지구를 돕는 방법

Bees carry pollen from flower to flower. This pollen goes from the male parts of the flowers to the female parts of the flowers. This is called pollination.
벌은 꽃에서 꽃으로 꽃가루를 옮겨요.
이 꽃가루는 꽃의 수컷부분에서 부터
암컷부분으로 갑니다. 이것을
수분이라고 해요.

Pollination helps plants make fruits and seeds. Fruits and seeds can grow into new plants. All of Earth's plants help to make air for life to survive.

수분은 식물이 과일과 씨를 만드는 것을 도와줘요. 과일과 씨는 새로운 식물을 만들 수 있어요. 지구에 있는 모든 식물은 생존을 위한 공기를 만들어 줘요.

How Bees Help Other Animals
벌이 다른 동물을 돕는 방법

Animals need plants to eat. Without bees, animals would be very hungry.
동물은 먹을 수 있는 식물이 필요해요. 벌이 없다면 동물들은 매우 배고플거에요.

Bees pollinate some of the most delicious foods on Earth. There would be less nuts, chocolate, and honey without bees.
벌들은 지구상의 가장 맛있는 음식들을 수분시켜줘요. 벌이 없다면 견과류, 초콜릿 그리고 꿀이 줄어들거에요.

How Bees Help Humans
벌이 사람을 돕는 방법

Bees make honey. Honey is very good for people to eat. It can help keep your body healthy.

벌은 꿀을 만들어요. 꿀은 사람에게 매우 좋죠. 꿀은 몸을 건강에도 좋아요.

Bumblebees only make a small amount of honey. They eat this honey themselves. Honeybees make enough honey for themselves and people to eat.
호박벌은 아주 적은 꿀밖에 못 만들어요. 호박벌들은 꿀을 만들어서 자기네들이 먹습니다. 꿀벌이 자기네들과 사람들이 먹을 수 있는 충분한 꿀을 만들어요.

Bees in Danger
멸종위기의 벌

Bees around the world are disappearing.
Scientists think climate change is one
reason this is happening.
전 세계의 벌이 사라지고 있어요. 과학자들은
기후변화때문이라고 생각해요.

Climate change is when a hot place
gets cooler, or a cool place gets hotter.
기후변화때문에 더운 곳은 시원해지고 시원한
곳은 더워져요.

Special chemicals called pesticides can get rid of weeds. Farmers use pesticides to protect their crops.
농약이라고 불리는 특별한 화학약품이 잡초를 없애요. 농부들은 작물을 보호하기위해 농약을 사용해요.

Pesticides are very dangerous to bees. Bees around the world are dying from pesticides.
농약은 벌에게 아주 위험해요. 전세계의 벌은 농약때문에 죽어가고 있어요.

How To Help Bees
벌을 돕는 방법

People can plant flowers that have a large amount of nectar in them. Bees like lavender, lilacs, and sunflowers.
사람들은 꿀이 많이 들어있는 꽃을 심을 수 있어요. 벌은 라벤더, 라일락 그리고 해바라기를 좋아해요.

You can make a "bee hotel" out of wood. This will attract bees to your garden. Bee hotels can keep bees safe and help their numbers grow.

숲에서 '벌 호텔'을 만들 수 있어요. 이렇게 해서 정원으로 벌을 유인할 수 있죠. 벌 호텔은 벌을 안전하게 지킬 수 있고 개체수를 늘리게 도울 수 있어요.

People can help bees by spraying their weeds with vinegar instead of chemicals.

사람들은 잡초에 화학약품 대신 식초를 뿌려 벌을 도울 수 있어요.

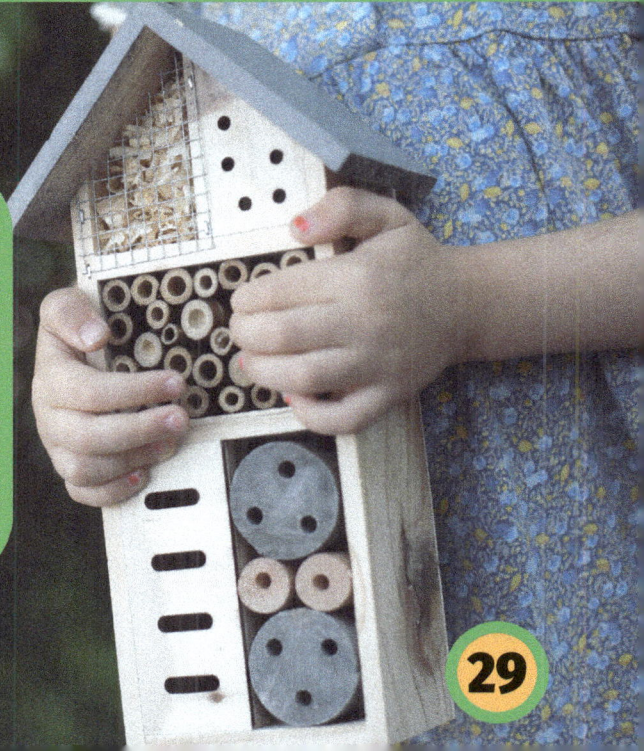

Quiz
퀴즈

Test your knowledge of bees by answering the following questions. The questions are based on what you have read in this book. The answers are listed on the bottom of the next page.

밑의 질문들에 대답을 하면서 박쥐에 대한 지식을 테스트 해보세요. 질문은 위에서 읽은 내용에 기초합니다. 정답은 다음 페이지에 적혀있어요.

1
How many legs do bees have?
벌의 다리는 몇개인가요?

2
What are the wires on a bee's head called?
벌의 머리에 있는 선은 무엇인가요?

3
What do killer bees do if they are upset?
살인벌이 화나면 무엇을 하나요?

4
What food do bees make?
벌은 어떤 음식을 만드나요?

5
What is climate change?
기후변화는 무엇인가요?

6
What flowers do bees like?
벌이 좋아하는 꽃은 무엇인가요?

Explore other books in the Animals That Make a Difference series.

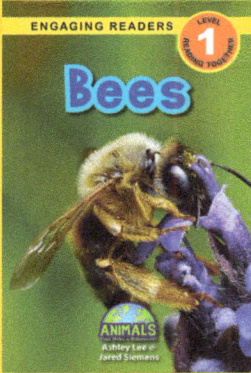

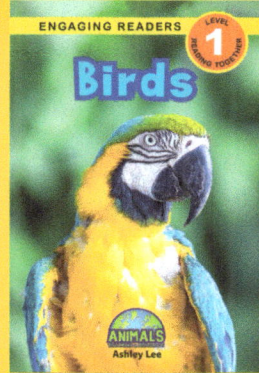

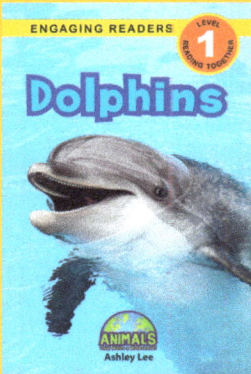

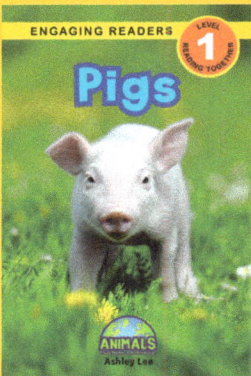

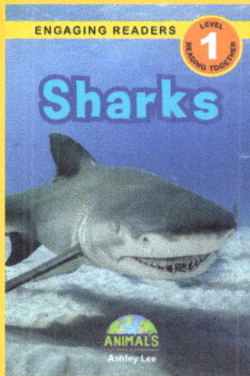

Visit www.engagebooks.com to explore more Engaging Readers.

1. 여섯개 2. 더듬이 3. 사람들을 쫓아가요 4. 꿀
5. 더운 곳이 시원해지고 시원한 곳은 더워져요 6. 라벤더, 라일락, 그리고 해바라기
정답:

Answers:
1. Six 2. Antennae 3. Chase people 4. Honey
5. When a hot place gets cooler, or a cool place gets hotter
6. Lavender, lilacs, and sunflowers